4 TH

JOKES FOR

KIDS

INDEPENDENCE DAY JOKES FOR KIDS

Printed Worldwide
First Printing, 2017
ISBN : 9781548033903

1.   **1.** **What did the colonists wear to the Boston Tea Party?**

Answer: Tea-shirts

2. **A teacher asks her young students what the last words to the Star Spangled Banner were.**

Little Johnny raises his hand and says, "Play Ball."

3. What's red, white, and blue?

Answer: A sad candy-cane.

4. Where was the Declaration of Independence signed?

Answer: At the bottom.

5. Teacher: More than 200 years ago, the American forefathers defeated the British in the Revolutionary War, thus winning our independence.

Student: Wow! They must have been really strong for only 4 of them to defeat and entire army!

6. What do you call an American drawing?

Answer: Yankee Doodle.

7. What did George Washington say to his men before crossing the Delaware?

Answer: "Well, you have to get in the boat guys."

8. Mother: "Ricky swallowed some of the firecrackers you gave him to fire tonight!"

Father: "Well, is he okay?"

Mother: "I really don't know, I haven't heard the last report yet."

9. When does Europe celebrate July 4th?

Answer: Right after July 3rd.

10. Why does the Statue of Liberty stand in New York Harbor?

Answer: Because she can't sit down.

11. What happened as a result of the famous Stamp Act?

Answer: The American's licked the British.

12. Why aren't there any knock knock jokes about America?

Answer: Because freedom rings.

13. What is red, white, black, and blue?

Answer: Uncle Sam falling down the stairs.

14. What kind of tea did the colonists want?

Answer: Liber-tea.

15. What was George Washington's favorite kind of tree?

Answer: infan-tree.

16. What was by far the most popular dance in 1776?

Answer: Indepen-dance.

17. Who was a notorious jokester in George Washington's army?

Answer: Lafayette.

18. Why did the duck say bang on July 4th?

Answer: Because he was shooting fire quackers.

19. What is the biggest difference between a duck and George Washington?

Answer: One has a bill on his face, the other is a face on a bill.

20. How were the American colonists like ants?

Answer: They lived in colonies.

21. What is a popular meal on July 5th?

Answer: Independence Day old pizza.

22. What quacks, has a bill, and betrays his country?

Answer: Beneduck Arnold.

23. What did the fuse say to the firecracker?

Answer: If we get together, we can pop it like it's hot.

24. What protest occurred in 1772 by a group of angry dogs?

Answer: The Boston Flea Party.

25. Why did Paul Revere ride his horse from Boston to Lexington?

Answer: Well, the horse was too heavy to carry.

26. Did you hear that great joke about the Liberty Bell?

Answer: Yes, it cracked me up.

27. What would you call a duck on the 4th of July?

Answer: A fire quacker.

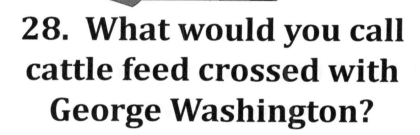

28. What would you call cattle feed crossed with George Washington?

Answer: The Fodder of Our Country.

29. What did one flag say to the other flag?

Answer: No talking necessary, it just waved.

30. Which colony told the most jokes?

Answer: Pun-Sylvania.

31. What is red, white, blue, and green?

Answer: A very patriotic turtle.

32. How is a healthy person like the United States?

Answer: They both have good constitutions.

33. What did King George think of the American Colonists?

Answer: He thought they were revolting.

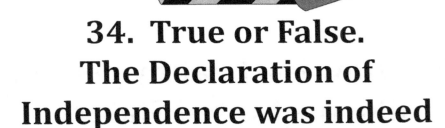

34. True or False. The Declaration of Independence was indeed written in Philadelphia?

Answer: False, it was actually written in ink.

35. Why did British soldiers wear red coats?

Answer: So they could hide in tomatoes.

36. What is red, white, blue, and ugly?

Answer: The Revolutionary Warthog.

37. How was the 4th of July picnic?

Answer: The hotdogs were pretty good, but the brats were the wurst.

38. What is red, white, blue, and green?

Answer: A patriotic pickle.

39. How is the Liberty Bell like a dropped Easter egg?

Answer: Because they are both cracked.

40. What is Uncle Sam's favorite snack?

Answer: Fire crackers.

41. What else is red, white, blue, and green?

Answer: A seasick Uncle Sam.

42. What do you call an American Revolutionary artist?

Answer: A Yankee doodler.

43. What was the craziest battle of the American Revolution?

Answer: The Battle of Bonkers Hill.

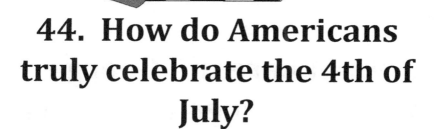

44. How do Americans truly celebrate the 4th of July?

Answer: By sitting in traffic for hours.

45. Nothing says "Happy July 4th" like eating too much candy and accidently throwing up over the neighbors dog

46. Where did George Washington go to buy his hatchet?

Answer: The chopping mall.

47. What do you get when you cross an American patriot with a small, curly-haired dog?

Answer: A Yankee Poodle.

48. What has feathers, webbed feet, and inalienable rights?

Answer: The Ducklaration of Independence.

49. What did one firecracker say to the other?

Answer: My pop is bigger than your pop.

50. What do you get when you cross a signer of the Declaration of Independence with a rooster?

Answer: John Hancock-a-doodle-doo.

51. What did the parrot named Polly want for the 4th of July?

Answer: A fire cracker.

52. What is red, white, blue, and yellow?

Answer: A star-spangled banana.

53. What did Paul Revere say as he arrived in Lexington after his famous ride?

Answer: I have got to get a softer saddle.

54. Why did George Washington chop down the cherry tree with his hatchet?

Answer: Because his mom said he couldn't use his chainsaw.

55. If you crossed a vegetable with our first president, what would you get?

Answer: George Squashington.

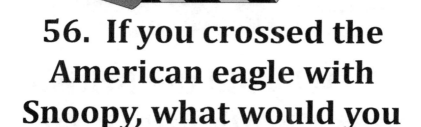

56. If you crossed the American eagle with Snoopy, what would you get?

Answer: A Bald Beagle.

57. If you crossed a founding father with a notable monster, what would you get?

Answer: Benjamin Franklinstein.

58. Why did the British cross the Atlantic Ocean?

Answer: To get to the other tide.

59. What did the patriot put on his dry, chapped skin?

Answer: Revo-lotion.

60. Who is most dog's favorite founding father?

Answer: Bone Franklin.

61. What did Washington ask as he crossed the Delaware River?

Answer: "How much were the reserved seats?"

62. Who was a fake patriot?

Answer: Uncle Sham.

63. If roaches and rats lived at George Washington's house, what would you call it?

Answer: Mt. Vermin.

64. What has four legs, a red nose, and fought for this British?

Answer: Rudolph the Red Coat Reindeer.

65. What cat warned the Minutemen that the British were coming?

Answer: Paw Revere.

66. What was Thomas Jefferson's favorite dessert?

Answer: Monti Jello.

67. What ghost haunted King George III?

Answer: The spirit of 1776.

68. What pig signed the Declaration of Independence?

Answer: John Hamcock.

69. Why did George Washington put a chicken on guard duty?

Answer: He wanted a chicken to catch a Tory.

70. What do you call a parade of German mercenaries?

Answer: A Hessian procession.

71. What do you get when you cross the first president with a dog?

Answer: George Washingtongue.

72. What is a hungry boy's favorite picnic event?

Answer: The snack race.

73. Why did Washington's army win the Battle of Trenton?

Answer: Because the enemy was Hessian around.

74. What would you get if you crossed a monster with a Washington officer?

Answer: Baron von Steupid.

75. Who wrote "Oh, say can you see?"

Answer: An eye doctor.

76. What did the Italian colonist say to the British soldier?

Answer: Give me lasagna, or give me death.

77. What did the tourist say as he left the Statue of Liberty?

Answer: "Keep in torch."

78. What's big, cracked, and carries your luggage?

Answer: The liberty bellhop.

79. What do you call a great American drawing by an American child?

Answer: A Yankee Doodle dandy.

80. How did the colonists decide on the flag?

Answer: They took a flag poll.

81. Why did Uncle Sam wear red, white, and blue suspenders?

Answer: To hold up his pants.

82. What famous person do you get when you make a wreath of $100 bills?

Answer: Aretha Franklin.

83. What did the little firecracker say to the big firecracker?

Answer: Hi, pop.

84. British people say American's go overboard with 4th of July celebrations. In reality, the only thing that went overboard was their tea.

85. What march would you play at a jungle parade?

Answer: Tarzan Stripes Forever.

86. What kind of dinosaur shoot fireworks on the 4th of July?

Answer: Dino-mite.

87. How is the American Flag like Santa Claus?

Answer: They both hang out on the pole.

88. What was the colonist's favorite cookie?

Answer: A flag newton.

89. What did George Washington say to his men at the Battle of Valley Forge?

Answer: "Sorry men, the flights to Florida are all booked."

90. Who gave the Liberty Bell to Philadelphia?

Answer: A duck family. It was all quacked

91. What is the best time to have a parade?

Answer: March.

92. What did the colonist put in his soup?

Answer: Firecrackers.

93. Chuck Norris doesn't celebrate the 4th of July. The 4th of July celebrates Chuck Norris.

94. What did the colonist's do at the Boston Tea Party?

Answer: I don't know, I wasn't invited.

95. Why did George Washington stand up in the boat as his men crossed the Delaware River?

Answer: He was afraid he would have to get an oar and row if he sat down.

96. What did Thomas Jefferson say when the founding fathers were reading off the Declaration of Independence?

Answer: More like pre-ramble. I am ready for lunch.

97. What did the dog do on Independence Day?

Answer: He flagged his tail.

98. What's red, white, blue, and gross?

Answer: Uncle Spam.

99. Why did Paul Revere take the Midnight Ride?

Answer: Because he missed the 10:30 P.M. bus.

100. Why did Paul Revere yell, "The Martians are coming?"

Answer: His horse had kicked him in the head.

Made in the USA
Middletown, DE
26 June 2022

67841882R00031